*Women's Basketball Drills
A Fundamental Approach to Winning*

OFFENSIVE DRILLS

by
Joan Bonvicini
*Head Basketball Coach
Long Beach State*

CHAMPIONSHIP BOOKS
P.O. Box 1166, ISU Station
Ames, Iowa 50010

© Copyright 1988 by Championship Books, Ames, Iowa
ISBN #0-932741-59-2

All rights reserved. No part of this book may be reproduced in any form by any means without permission in writing from the publisher.

PRINTED IN THE UNITED STATES OF AMERICA

Dedication

To my assistant coaches, my ball players, and most of all my family.

About the Author

Few collegiate coaches can match the impressive record Joan Bonvicini has achieved in just nine seasons at Long Beach State University.

In 1988 her 49ers advanced to their second straight Final Four appearance, finishing with a 28-6 record and No. 7 national ranking. In her nine years at Long Beach, Bonvicini has won eight conference championships and compiled a record of 246-49, a winning percentage of .834. Each of her teams has won at least 24 games a season!

Known as an outstanding recruiter, Bonvicini was honored after the 1980-81 season as the NCAA Division I Coach of the Year. She is active on the national circuit as a speaker and clinician and served as President of the Women's Basketball Coaches Association. She has also traveled to Italy as a guest instructor in 1984.

She is a 1975 graduate of Southern Connecticut State, where she was herself a star guard.

Table of Contents

Three-on-Three Continuous 1
Baseball Outlet Drill 2
Overhead Chest Pass (Tossback)......................... 3
Four Player Rebound/Transition 4
Five Player Weave/Three-on-Two 5
Three Line Fastbreak 6
Three-on-Two/Two-on-One 7
Three Player Rebound/Transition 8
Tossback Rotation Passing 9
Continuous Rebounding..................................10
Rebound Outlet 11
Post Feed Drill 12
Snake Drill 13
Two Line Passing..14
Toughness Drill 15
Monkey in the Middle 16
Monster Rebounding 17
Two Line Fastbreak 18
Mirror Dribbling 19
Jump Stop/Pivot 20
"L" Cut/Square Up......................................21
Three Line Footwork 22
Ball Rolls 23
Tipping Drill 24
Fireman Drill 25
Ante-Over Drill 26
Four Player Shell Drill 27
Three Player Shell Drill 28
Screen and Roll 29
Give and Go 30
Penetrate Seam/Kickout 31
Obstacle Dribbling 32
Dribble Tag 33
Two-on-One Decision Drill 34
One-on-One Post Drill 35
Elimination One-on-One 36
Transition "Clear" 37
One-on-One Half Court 38
Three Player Weave/Three Shots 39
Three Player Spot Shooting 40

Knock-out Shooting	41
Breakaway Layup Drill	42
Three Player Chase and Shoot	43
Beat Dr. "J" Shooting	44
"Mikan" Drill	45
Partner Free Throws	46
Competitive Free Throws	47
Team Free Throws	48
Reverse Dribble/Power Layup	49
Short "17"	50
Tossback Shooting	51
Full Court Shooting	52
Big Post Drill	53
Post Shooting	54
Contest the Shooter/Rebound	55
Reaction Shooting	56
Twenty-One	57
Three Player/Two Ball Shooting	58

Name of Drill: THREE-ON-THREE CONTINUOUS
Use throughout the season

PURPOSE: Live fastbreak drill. Provides passing, dribbling, shooting, defense and conditioning.

Player 1 tosses the ball off the backboard and runs a three player break against two defenders, 8 and 9. If 8 or 9 rebound, they outlet to player 10. They run a three player break against 4 and 5. This drill is continuous and players fill in when they finish their offensive series. They either enter the outlet line or play tandem defense.

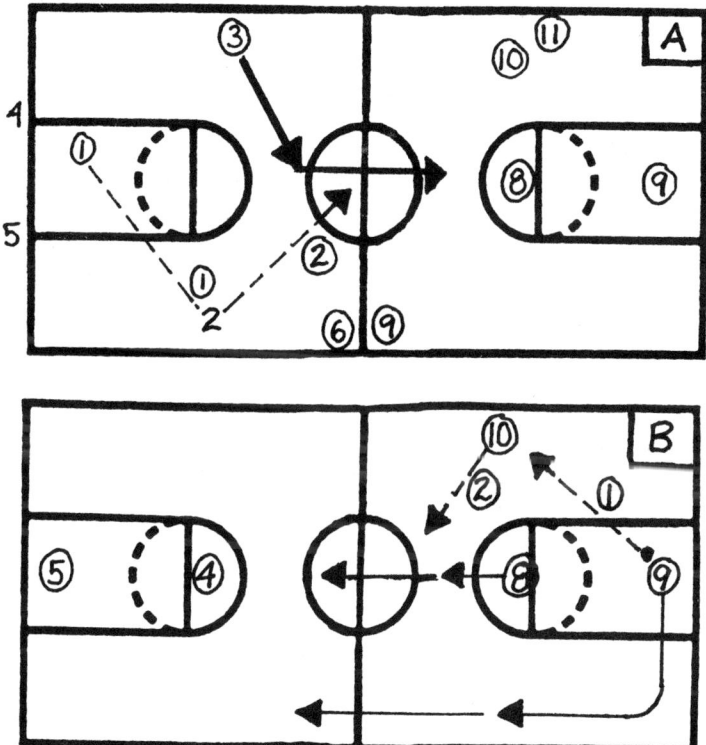

COACHING POINTS: Excellent conditioning drill. Forces players to think and react while they are tired. Allow no more than three passes when they cross half court. Run the drill for two minutes and increase up to five minutes.

Name of Drill: BASEBALL OUTLET DRILL

Use throughout the season

PURPOSE: Teaches the rebounder to throw the long outlet pass. Teaches outlet to sprint and shoot.

Divide the team into three lines of rebounders and outlets. There will be a coach at each free throw line. The drill begins with players 1 and 7 getting the rebound off the board and throwing a baseball pass to either player 4 or 10. They catch and dribble then pass to the coach. The coach passes back and they shoot either a layup or jump shot. The next rebounder in line gets the ball out of the basket and passes to either player 5 or 11. After rebounding they go to the outlet line, the outlet to the rebounding line.

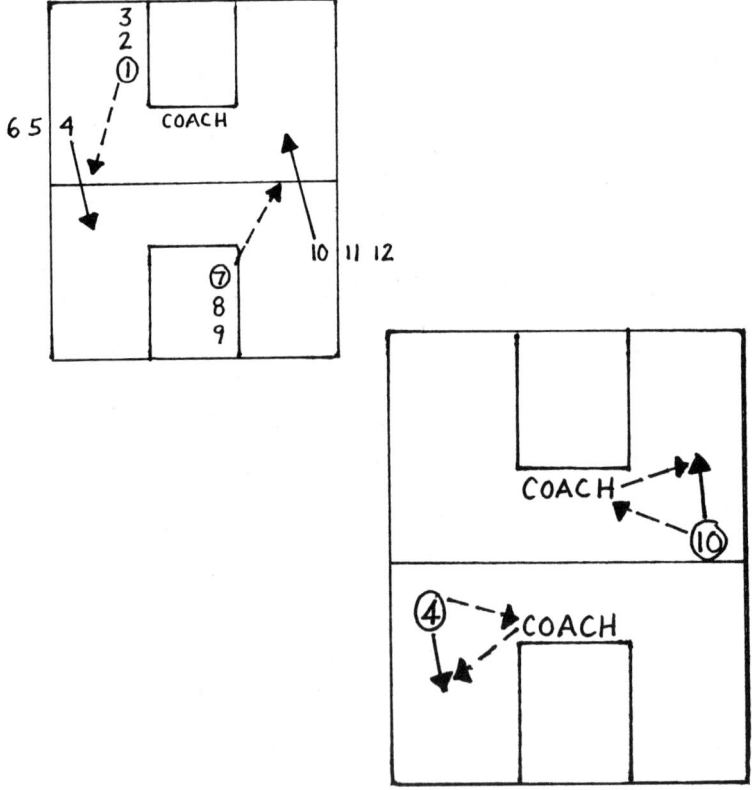

COACHING POINTS: Throw a good baseball pass and catch it on the run.

Name of Drill: OVERHEAD CHEST PASS (TOSSBACK)
Use pre-season

PURPOSE: Teaches overhead chest pass after a rebound.

The ball is passed with authority with an overhead pass. Full arm extension is required. Ball is passed with the wrists. Throw rapidly, always catching the ball.

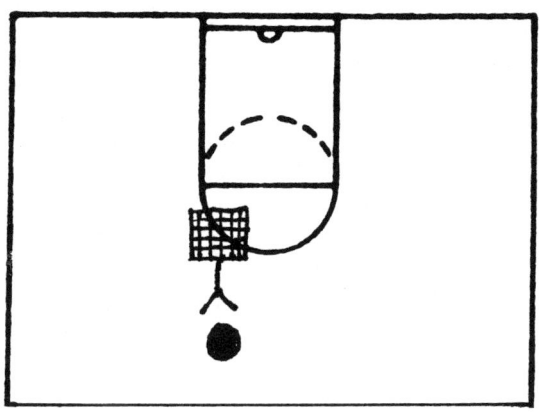

COACHING POINTS: Fifty passes or sixty seconds. Do not bat ball.

Name of Drill: FOUR PLAYER REBOUND/TRANSITION

Use throughout the season

PURPOSE: Works on shooting, rebounding and running the break.

Divide the team into groups of four. Four players on offense will be guarded by four defensive players. A coach has the ball and will pass to one of the offensive players, who will shoot. If the basket is made, she stays and the coach passes again. If it is missed, defense will run a transition break against players 1, 2, 3 and 4. At the end of the made shot or rebound, defense steps off and new defensive players come on the court.

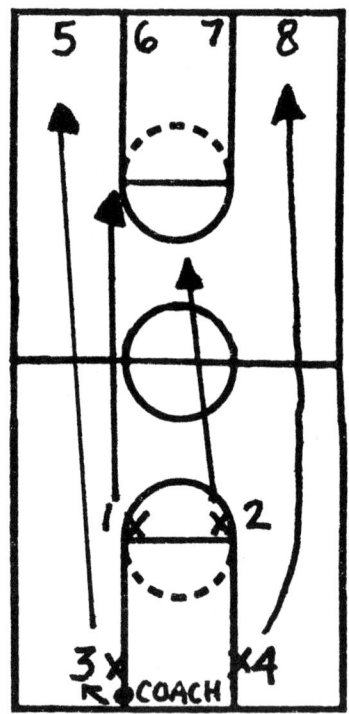

COACHING POINTS: Only run transition on a defensive rebound. Live drill can be more competitive if the coach keeps statistics on each team.

Name of Drill: FIVE PLAYER WEAVE/THREE-ON-TWO
Use throughout the season

PURPOSE: Improves passing and transition from offense to defense.

Divide the teams into groups of five. Start the ball in the middle and chest pass and weave to the free throw line. Do a bounce pass layup. Always pass and go behind to the end. The shooter and the last passer will be the two defensive players. The three offensive players will be 1, 3 and 4.

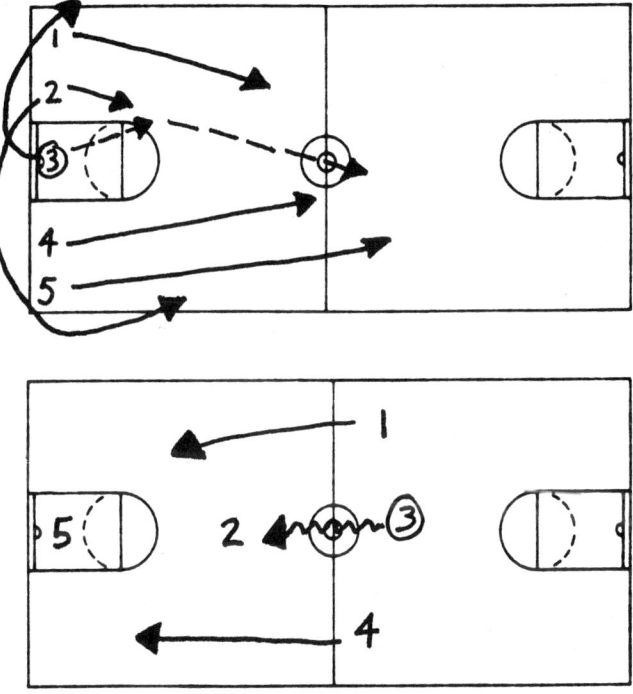

COACHING POINTS: Give a good chest pass and sprint ahead but behind players. Run as quickly as possible from offense to defense.

Name of Drill: THREE LINE FASTBREAK
Use throughout the season

PURPOSE: Improves techniques of fastbreak and transition.

Divide the team into three lines. The first three players step up with player 1 being the rebounder, player 2 the outlet and player 3 the middle. The coach will toss the ball off the basket with player 1 rebounding and yelling "ball." The player will throw an outlet pass to player 2. Player 2 will then make a chest pass to player 3 who yells "middle." Player 1 will fill the lane opposite the pass. A coach will be at the opposite free throw line to force a jump stop. Each group must do these drills:

1. jump stop—bounce pass, layup
2. jump stop, chest pass, jump shot
3. jump stop—chest pass fake away, pass back to the point, jump shot

Once the three shoot, rebound and put the shot in the basket, sprint back and go to the end of a different line.

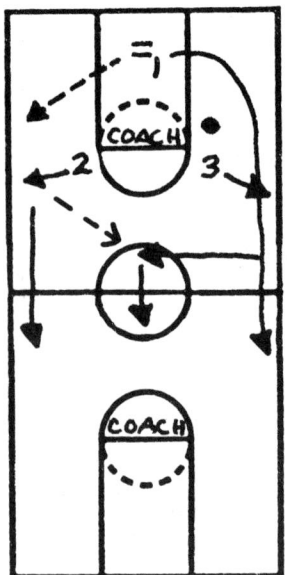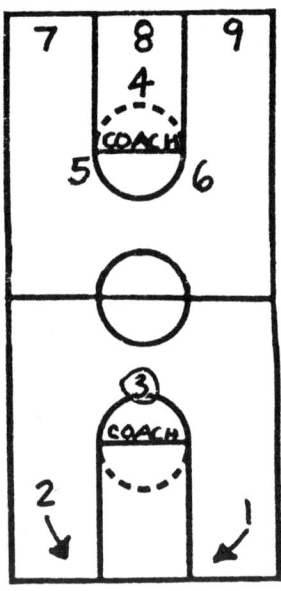

COACHING POINTS: Watch passing and jump stop fundamentals. Execute correctly but don't hurry.

Name of Drill: THREE-ON-TWO/TWO-ON-ONE
Use throughout the season

PURPOSE: Teaches a live fastbreak drill.

Divide the team into groups of three. Put two defenders out of bounds at half court. Run a three line fastbreak with the coach tossing the ball off the basket. Once the rebound is secure, 4 and 5 slap hands in the middle of the court and play a tandem defense. Players 1, 2 and 3 will continue down court. No more than three passes are attempted once crossing half court. If a shot is made or players 4 or 5 rebound, the shooter will now be the defense and player 4 and 5 the offense. They will proceed to the other end of the court and score against player 1. Players 2 and 3 will become the new defensive players at half court and 7, 8 and 9 will start the drill again.

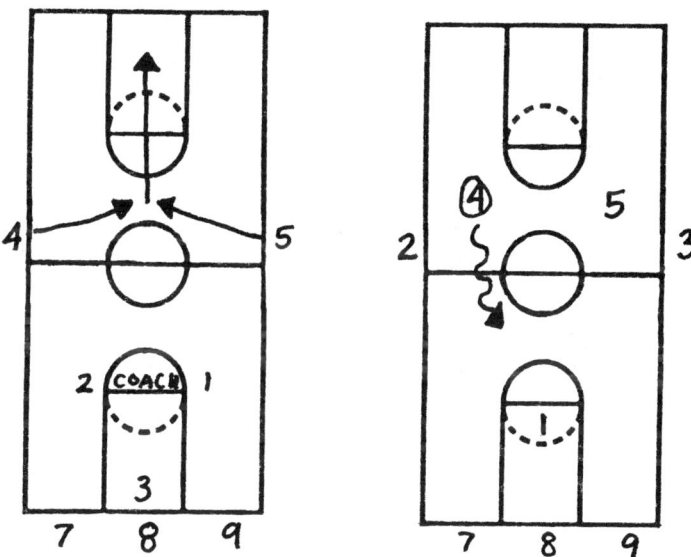

COACHING POINTS: Work on tandem defense. Bottom player follows the pass. Two-on-one return players should always get a layup.

Name of Drill: THREE PLAYER REBOUND/TRANSITION

Use throughout the season

PURPOSE: This drill works on shooting, rebounding and running the break.

Divide the team into groups of three with each having a guard, forward and a center. Three players on offense 1, 2 and 3 will be guarded by defense. The coach will pass the ball to the offense, which will shoot. If the defense rebounds the ball, they will run a transition break (rebound, outlet, middle) against players 1, 2 and 3. Defense will step off and a new defensive team comes on the court.

COACHING POINTS: If the offense shoots and makes a basket, it stays. Only run transition on a defensive rebound. Makes both teams run the transition, block out and go to the basket.

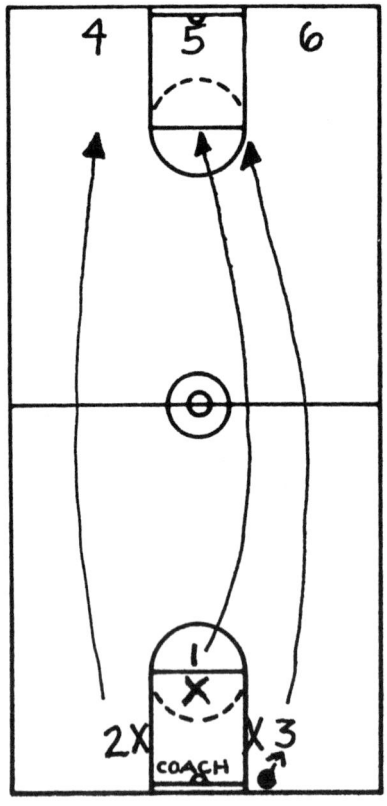

Name of Drill: TOSSBACK ROTATION PASSING
Use throughout the season

PURPOSE: To increase strength in passing and footwork.

Line three players next to each other facing a tossback. The middle player has the ball and will chest pass and move to the right. Player 3 will catch and pass and move to the left. Player 1 will catch and pass and move to the right. Always catch and move behind teammates.

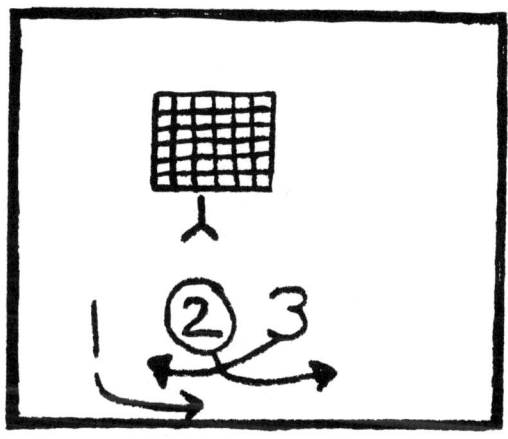

COACHING POINTS: Use a tip pass or a chest pass. Play hard by competing how many passes can be completed in 30 seconds.

Name of Drill: CONTINUOUS REBOUNDING
Use throughout the season

PURPOSE: Works on offensive rebound/outlet.

Line team up facing the backboard. The first two players in line have a ball. There is a player on the outlet. The first player gives the ball quickly to the coach, who tosses the ball off the backboard. Player 1 will rebound and outlet to player 7. Player 7 will pass to player 3. Player 1 will be the new outlet. The drill will proceed very quickly until everyone goes through twice. The coach moves to the left side of the court.

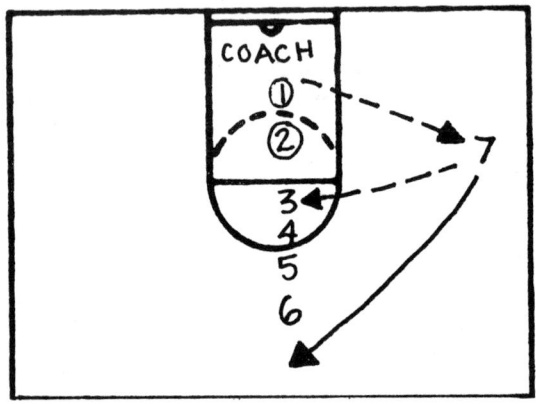

COACHING POINTS: Use only the overhead outlet pass. Yell "ball" and "outlet."

Name of Drill: REBOUND OUTLET
Use throughout the season

PURPOSE: Works on offensive rebounding and outletting.

Divide the team into two lines facing the basket with two outlets on opposite sides. On the whistle, players 1 and 5 will throw the ball off the backboard, rebound and yell "ball." The players will outlet to their side of the court. Player 9 will chest pass to player 2, player 10 will chest pass to player 6. Go to the end of the opposite line. The rebounder becomes the new outlet. The players should concentrate on these fundamentals:

1. Rebound and spread legs (spread eagle)
2. Pivot on the outside foot
3. ONLY overhead outlet passes
4. Be quick, no turnovers

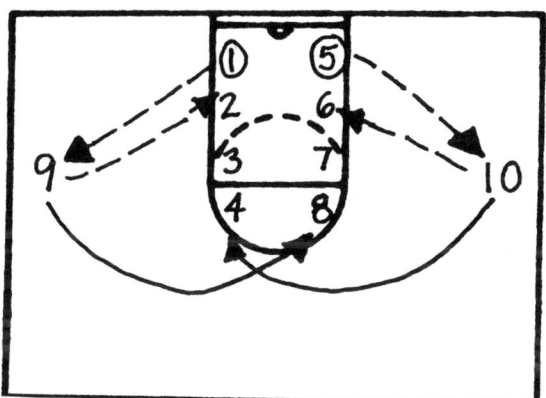

COACHING POINTS: Watch rebounders pivot foot and force the players to yell "ball" and "outlet." The drill should move quickly. Outlet should have her back to the sideline and yell "outlet."

Name of Drill: POST FEED DRILL
Use throughout the season

PURPOSE: Improves passes to the post from the perimeter. Read the defense.

Line three players on offense and three players on defense on the perimeter. Post up on the block with defense on the block. A wing player will have the ball and attempt to pass to the post. If she has a shot, the post will take it, if not, throw it back to the perimeter. If the post is not open, pass the ball to a different perimeter player.

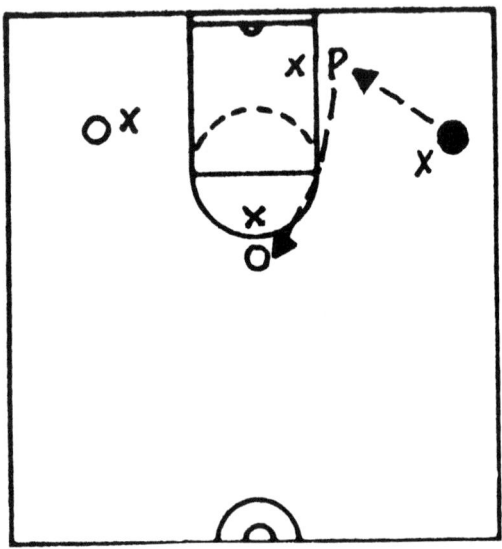

COACHING POINTS: This is an excellent drill which combines passing, defense and offensive post moves. Defense works hard on perimeter passing. Post will rotate after 30 seconds from offense to defense. Rotate perimeter positions.

Name of Drill: SNAKE DRILL

Use in pre-practice warmup

PURPOSE: This drill loosens the team up and works on passing on the move.

Divide the team into partners with two lines at each end of the court. One partner has the ball and on the whistle will jog the pass back and forth on the move.
1. chest pass
2. bounce pass
3. two dribble chest pass
4. two dribble bounce pass

When each group gets to the end of the court, they will go to the end of the opposite line. Don't start until the group in front reaches half court.

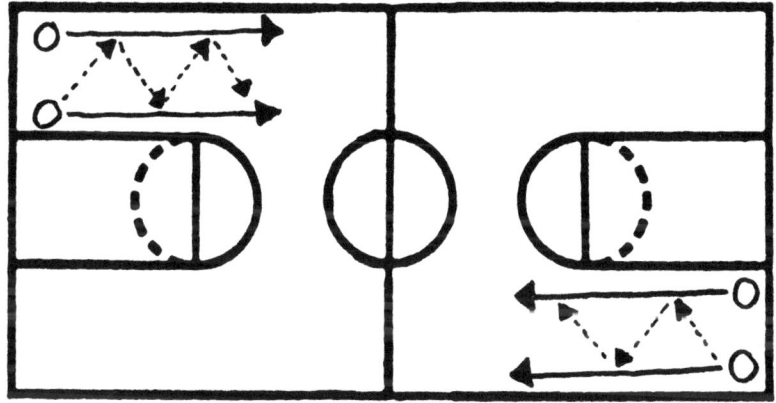

COACHING POINTS: Each group should go up and down the court before changing the passing. Have hands ready to receive the pass when jogging.

Name of Drill: TWO LINE PASSING
Use pre-season

PURPOSE: Quicken reaction to a chest or bounce pass.

Divide the team into pairs facing each other 12 to 15 feet away. Each player has a ball. The players to the right will chest pass; the players to the left will bounce pass. On the whistle, all players will pass (either chest or bounce) and execute correctly. On the whistle the lines will switch, bounce to chest pass, chest to bounce pass. This will help their reaction time. Blow the whistle again and they reverse back.

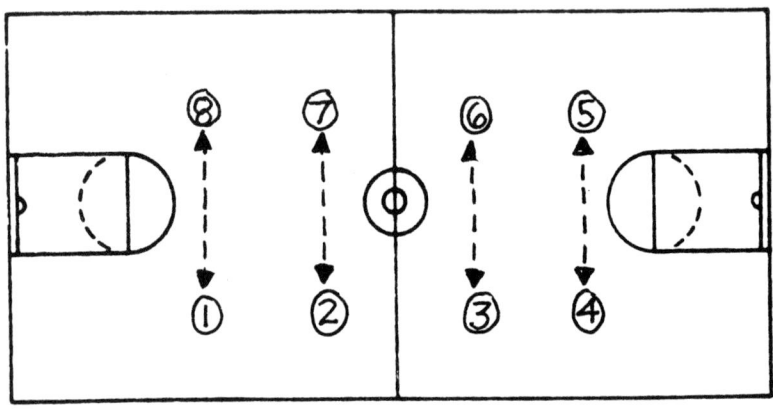

COACHING POINTS: Work on executing passes correctly (thumbs down, step through, etc.). Stress quickness.

Name of Drill: TOUGHNESS DRILL

Use in pre-season

PURPOSE: Increases aggressiveness to dive and retrieve a loose ball.

Divide the team into pairs by speed and quickness. A coach has a ball and the first two players are facing the coach with their backs to the basket. The coach will roll the ball down the middle of the court and on the word "go" both players will dive and retrieve the ball. Whoever gets there first will then drive to the basket for a shot with the other playing defense. The drill is completed when a shot is made or defense gets the rebound.

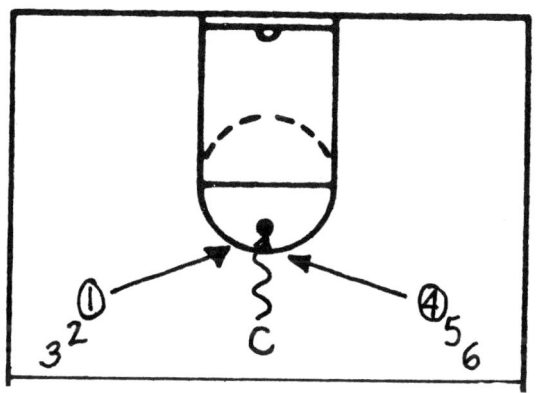

COACHING POINTS: This is a very physical drill. Watch for flagrant fouls. Let the players be physical without hurting each other.

Name of Drill: MONKEY IN THE MIDDLE
Use throughout the season

PURPOSE: To improve passing under pressure.

Divide the team into groups of three by height. Two players are on offense, one player is on defense. The player with the ball is being guarded by a defensive player and must pass the ball to the partner 12 to 15 feet away. The player can't pass until the defense is closely guarding the offense. The coach allows all types of passes *except* lob passes. Players should work on crisp passing, faking high, throwing low, etc. The coach will whistle to rotate spots after approximately 30 seconds.

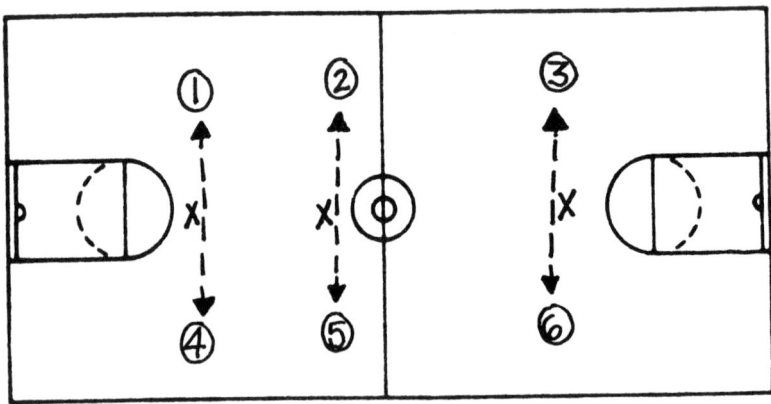

COACHING POINTS: Really work on teaching players to fake before passing. Use bounce passes, step-arounds, etc.

Name of Drill: MONSTER REBOUNDING
Use throughout the season

PURPOSE: Improves offensive rebounding without dribbling.

Divide the team into groups of three by height. A coach will be at the top of the key with a ball and the three players will line up across the free throw line facing the coach. The coach will shoot the ball and call "shot." All three players will go for the rebound and attempt to put the ball back in the basket. The following rules apply:

1. The first person to three points wins
2. No dribbling
3. No flagrant fouls
4. Rebound outside of the paint is a dead ball

The coach will continue to shoot every time there is a basket made or a dead ball. The two losing players will perform pushups.

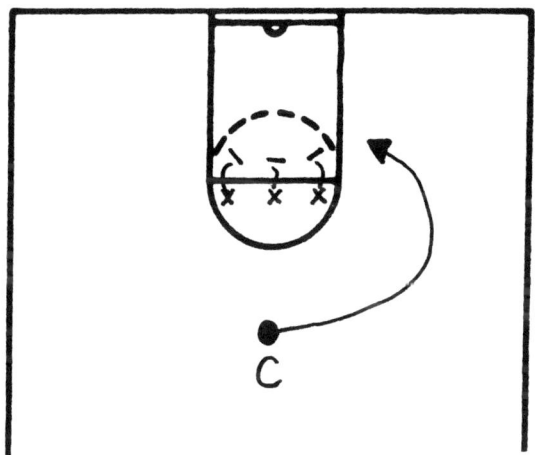

COACHING POINTS: This is a great rebounding drill because it is competitive and very physical. Don't let the players' fouling get out of hand. No dribbling—use head fakes.

Name of Drill: TWO LINE FASTBREAK

Use pre-season

PURPOSE: Teaches the beginning of a fastbreak with options.

Divide the team into groups of three. Three players at each outlet and three players at each end of the court. Players 4 and 10 each have a ball and are the rebound line. Players 1 and 7 are the outlet and shooting line. On the whistle, the first players in the rebound line will throw the ball against the backboard, rebound it and outlet to either player 1 or 7. They then do the following:

1. layup
2. jump stop, bounce pass, layup
3. jump stop, chest pass, bank shot
4. jump stop, chest pass, give and go

The rebounder will always follow and go to the right outside lane. Before the player advances to the next series of drills, be sure the players do the drill correctly. They will then go to the end of the line.

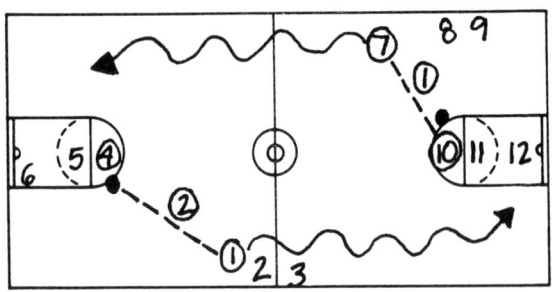

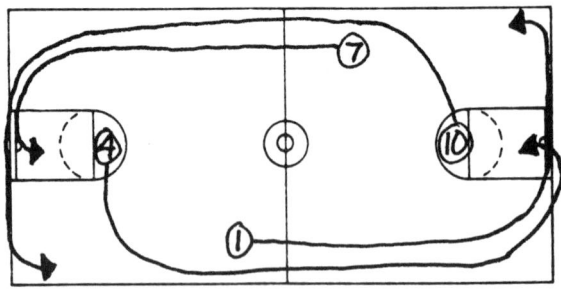

COACHING POINTS: Concentrate on the fundamentals (jump stops, filling the lanes, give and go fake). Be quick but don't hurry.

Name of Drill: MIRROR DRIBBLING

Use in pre-season

PURPOSE: Improves ball handling skills.

Spread the team out over half court and face the coach. Everyone will have a ball and do the following drills.

1. Pass ball around head
2. Pass ball around shoulders
3. Pass ball around waist
4. Pass ball around knees
5. Pass ball around feet
6. Figure eights/no dribble
7. Figure eights with dribble
8. Right hand dribble
9. Left hand dribble
10. Crossover in front
11. Crossover between legs
12. Crossover behind back
13. Laydown and dribble
14. Close eyes and dribble

The coach will demonstrate and all the players will follow.

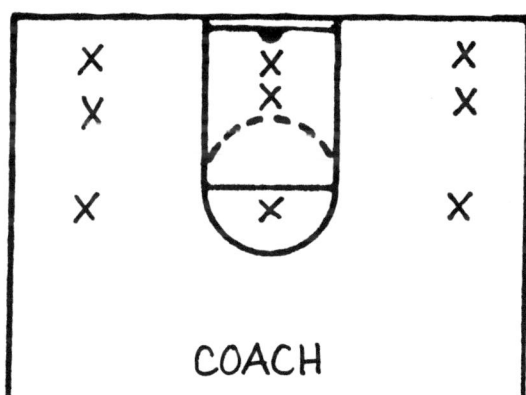

COACHING POINTS: Be sure to keep head up when dribbling. Protect the ball with the body.

Name of Drill: JUMP STOP/PIVOT

Use throughout the season

PURPOSE: Improves footwork and positioning.

Divide the team into three lines and have them jog to the free throw line extended and do:

1. Jump stop
2. Jump stop/right foot reverse pivot
3. Jump stop/left foot reverse pivot

After each player completes the assignment, the player will go to the end of the line. Each drill should be done twice.

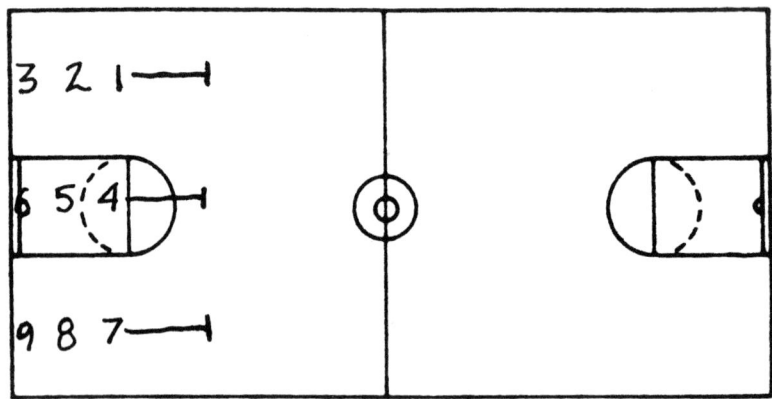

COACHING POINTS: The coach should watch that jump stops are executed properly with the knees bent in a crouch position.

Name of Drill: "L" CUTS/SQUARE UP

Use throughout the season

PURPOSE: Improves the players' movement without the ball.

Divide the players into two lines under the basket. Two coaches are at the top of the key with balls. The first player in each line will do an "L" cut and then go backdoor. Everyone goes through the drill twice. Once the player gets open on the wing, the coach will pass the ball and the offensive player will pivot on the inside foot and square up to the basket. The player will then pass the ball back to the coach and to the end of the line.

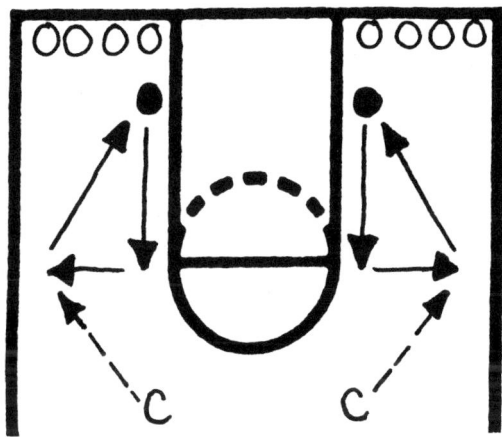

COACHING POINTS: The players should work hard to get open by varying speed. Don't try to shorten the "L" cut. When the player receives the pass, "square up" and put the ball on the hip. As the season progresses, add defense.

Name of Drill: THREE LINE FOOTWORK
Use at the beginning of practice

PURPOSE: This drill improves footwork and timing.

Divide the team into three lines and stand behind the baseline. On the whistle, the players will do the following:
1. Change of pace (jog, sprint)
2. Change of directions
3. Defensive slides
4. Backwards to half court (sprint)
5. Jump stop

Each player will run to the free throw line extended and do the exercise as assigned. The player shouldn't start until the person in front reaches the free throw line.

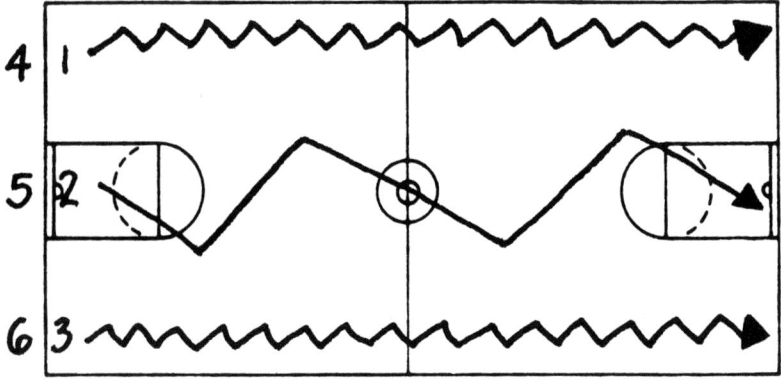

COACHING POINTS: Depending on the drill, whistle at the free throw line extended, half court, and free throw line (jog, sprint, jog). Work on form. Every drill is done twice.

Name of Drill: BALL ROLLS
Use throughout the season

PURPOSE: Improves passing, conditioning and footwork.

Divide team into pairs with one ball each. They should be a maximum of ten feet from their partner. The player with the ball will roll to her partner and throw a chest pass back. The passer will roll the ball quickly forcing her partner to move and slide. Each player does ten passes and switches spots.

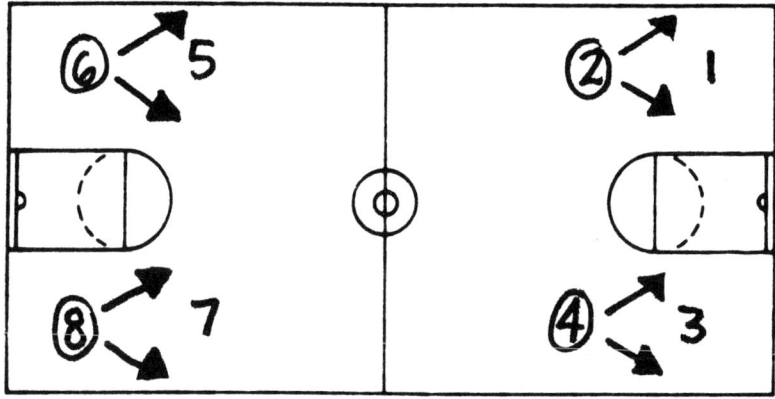

COACHING POINTS: Make sure the players roll the ball and force their teammates to move and slide. No crossing feet.

Name of Drill: TIPPING DRILL

Use throughout the season

PURPOSE: The drill improves strength and timing.

Divide the team into groups of three with one ball at each basket. On the whistle, each player will tip the ball according to the following instructions and go to the end of the line.
1. Right hand tip
2. Left hand tip
3. Two right hand tips
4. Two left hand tips
5. Two tips each, person behind tips in the basket

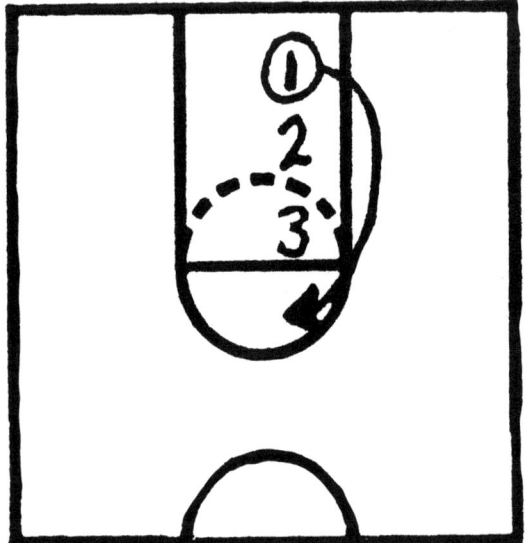

COACHING POINTS: The drill forces the players to tip the ball at the peak of their jump. The tipped ball must be at the rim level. If the player can't tip with the left hand, use both hands.

Name of Drill: FIREMAN DRILL
Use throughout the season

PURPOSE: Divide the team evenly into two lines facing each backboard. The first person in each line has a ball. On the whistle, each player will tip the ball off the backboard and sprint to the end of the opposite line. The ball must never touch the ground. Start at 30 seconds and increase the time as the season progresses. The maximum time should be 60 seconds.

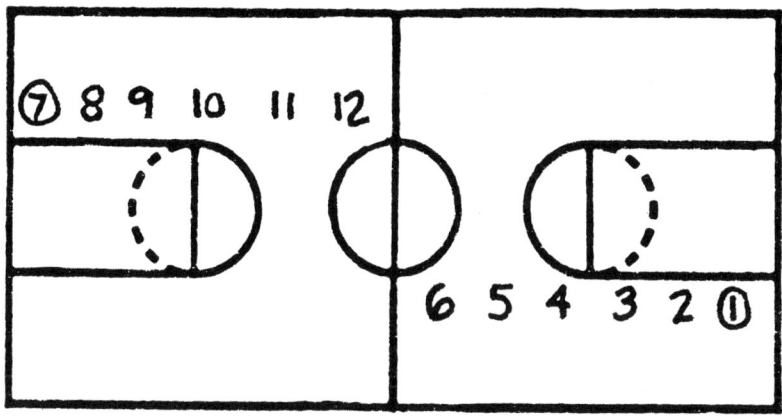

COACHING POINTS: Use two hand tipping and evolve to one hand. Run the drill on the left side of the court.

Name of Drill: ANTE-OVER DRILL
Use throughout the season

PURPOSE: Increases strength and timing.

Divide the team into groups of four to a basket with one ball. Player A has the ball and throws it off the backboard and goes behind player D. Player C tips the ball off the backboard to Player B and Player C goes behind Player B. Each player tips the ball ten times.

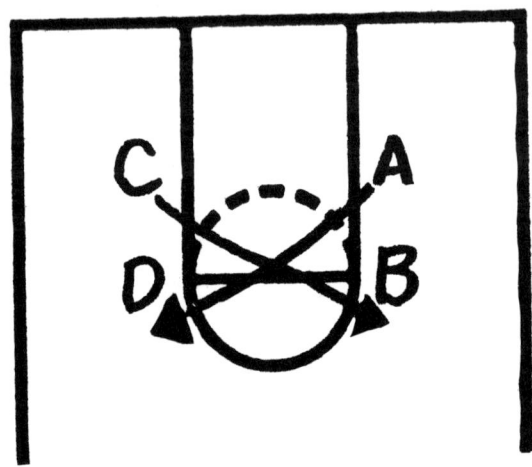

COACHING POINTS: If the ball is mishandled or is dropped, the drill starts from the beginning. Use two hand tipping and advance to one hand.

Name of Drill: FOUR PLAYER SHELL DRILL
Use throughout the season

PURPOSE: Improves every offensive and defensive area of half court basketball.

Use four players on offense and four players on defense. Each team is allowed four possessions on offense and they must pass a minimum of five times before a shot is attempted.
1. Give and go
2. Pass down, screen across
3. Pass across, screen down
4. Screen on the ball
5. Player replaces self
6. Get hand off back

Keep the court spread with 12 to 15 feet between each offensive player. The coach should keep track of shots made, rebounds turnovers, etc.

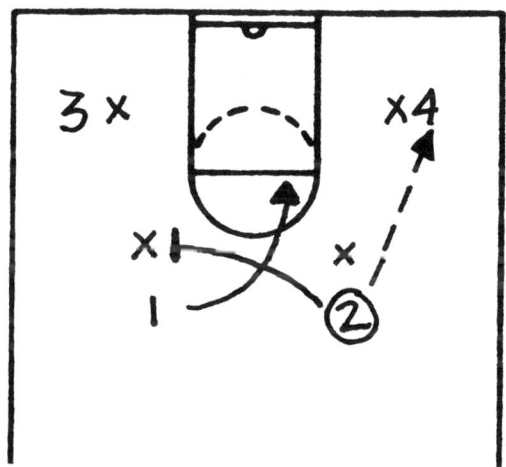

COACHING POINTS: This drill is a great conditioner. It forces players to play as hard as possible. The losing team by statistics must run laps.

Name of Drill: THREE PLAYER SHELL DRILL

Use throughout the season

PURPOSE: Improves passing, cutting and screening.

Divide the team into groups of three. Three will be on offense and three will be on defense. Offense has the ball and must do five passes before attempting a shot. Their options are:

1. Give and go
2. Screen away
3. Screen on the ball
4. Get hand off back
5. Player replaces self

At the beginning of the practice season, use "dummy" defense. As the season progresses, make the drill more competitive as to the number of shots made, turnovers, and rebounds. Keep track of each team's statistics.

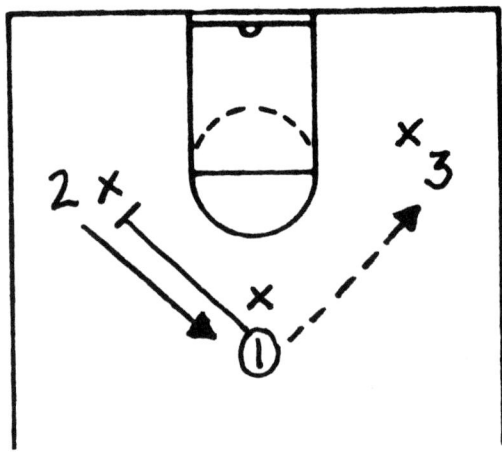

COACHING POINTS: This should be a very competitive drill. Divide the teams evenly and rotate offense to defense.

Name of Drill: SCREEN AND ROLL
Use throughout the season

PURPOSE: Divide the team into a line at the top of the key with one offensive and defensive player on the wing. The player with the ball will pass to the wing, fake away, then set a screen on the defensive player. The offensive wing will dribble once using the screen, then pass to the screener after the screener opens up and continues to the basket for a shot.

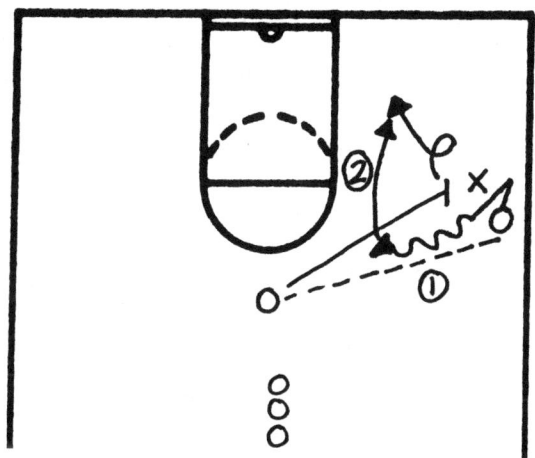

COACHING POINTS: The screeners should protect themselves by crossing their arms in front of their chest. The player will always know which way to open up by watching the ball handler. The player drives by her right side, opens with right foot and arm. When everyone goes through twice, use the drill on the left side of the court.

Name of Drill: GIVE AND GO
Use throughout the season

PURPOSE: Teaches the use of fakes and getting open without the ball.

Divide the team into two lines with guards at the top of the key with a ball, forwards and centers on the wing. A coach will be at the free throw line. The guard at the top will pass to a wing. The player then fakes away in front of the coach and cuts to the basket. The wing with the ball will either make a bounce pass or chest pass to the player cutting to the basket. The player then goes to the end of the opposite line.

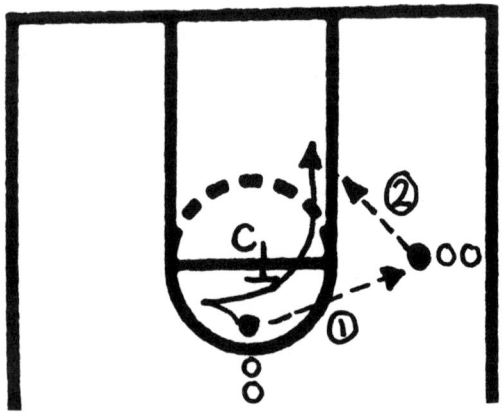

COACHING POINTS: Make sure the players make a good fake before cutting to the basket. As players use the drill more often, add defense.

Name of Drill: PENETRATE SEAM/KICKOUT
Use throughout the season

PURPOSE: Put three players on defense in a triangle and four players on offense in the seams. An offensive player with the ball will dribble and drive to the basket. Two defensive players will double team the ball handler. The ball handler must then pass to another offensive player who is open. The defense sets itself again and the offensive player again dribbles and drives to the basket.

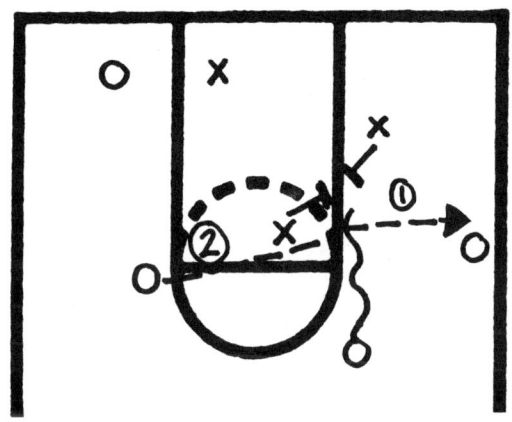

COACHING POINTS: Make sure that each offensive player has a chance to drive to the basket. As the drill progresses, the offensive player with the return pass can take the open jump shot.

Name of Drill: OBSTACLE DRIBBLING
Use pre-season

PURPOSE: Divide the team into two lines at opposite ends of the court. Everyone has a ball. Put eight cones at the foul line, half court, etc., on both sides. On the whistle the first player at each end dribbles to each cone and in order does these moves:

1. Cross-over dribble
2. Reverse dribble
3. Behind the back dribble
4. Between the legs dribble

The second player in line does not start until the first player reaches the second cone. Players go to the end of the opposite line and go again.

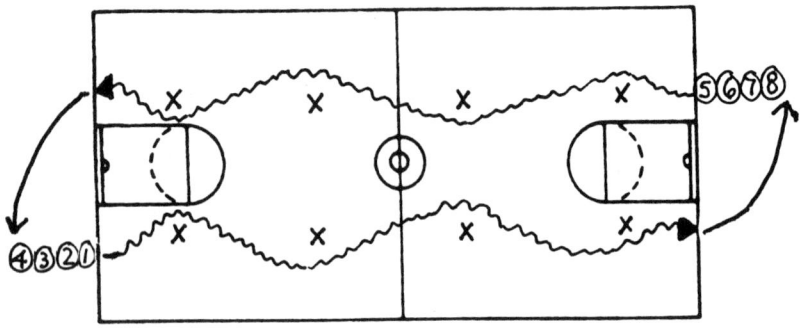

COACHING POINTS: Replace the cones with coaches or players. As the player dribbles, attempt to reach or steal the ball.

Name of Drill: DRIBBLE TAG

Use pre-season

PURPOSE: Each player has a ball and is in a set area on the court (one quarter of the basketball court). On the whistle, each player will dribble with her right hand only and try to steal or tip the ball away from the other players. The last player left dribbling is the winner. Do the same drill using only the left hand.

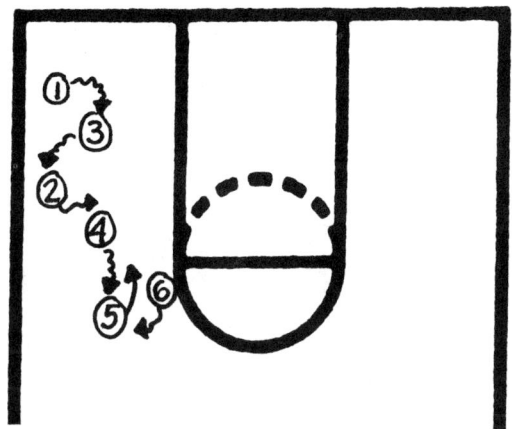

COACHING POINTS: As the game progresses and gets down to two players, confine the dribbling to a smaller area (free throw area).

Name of Drill: TWO-ON-ONE DECISION DRILL
Use throughout the season

PURPOSE: Forces the ball handler to make a decision to pass or shoot.

Divide the team into two lines. The line on the right has the balls. A coach is playing defense at the free throw line. Player 1 dribbles hard in a two-on-one situation with player 5 as a partner. Player 1 must read the defense to either shoot the ball for a layup or pass to player 5 for a layup. The players go to the end of the line on the opposite line.

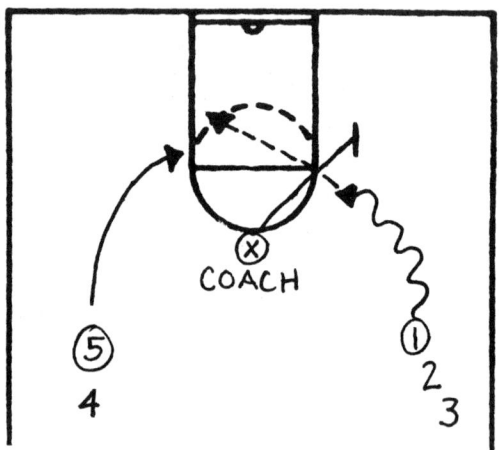

COACHING POINTS: The coach playing defense needs to work on faking at the ball handler to force a shot or playing the ball handler to force a pass. All teams must go full speed. Everyone goes through twice. Put the balls in the left hand line. No jump shots are allowed.

Name of Drill: ONE-ON-ONE POST DRILL
Use throughout the season

PURPOSE: Improves the offensive post and the player's individual moves. Makes the post read the defense.

Divide the team into partners by position. The first two players on the floor will position themselves on the low post block; one on offense and the other on defense. Two coaches will be on the court, the wing and the top of the key. The drill starts with the coach passing to the offensive post. If the player can get a good shot off, fine. If not, the player throws the ball back out to either coach and gets open again. The drill ends when a basket is made or the defense rebounds. Each player should get two or three attempts to shoot before rotating and the offense will go to defense. New offensive players come in.

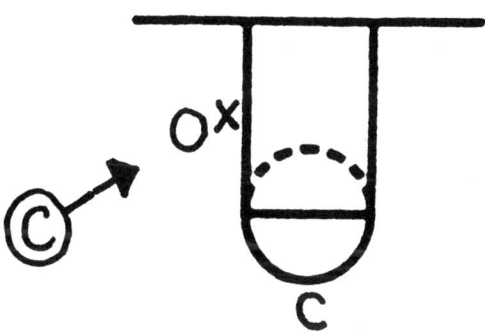

COACHING POINTS: Make the offensive player read the defense to get open. The player should always take a percentage shot. Follow every shot with a rebound. When everyone goes through twice, move the drill to the opposite side of the court.

Name of Drill: ELIMINATION ONE-ON-ONE
Use throughout the season

PURPOSE: Competitive one-on-one drill by position.

Divide the team into groups by position (guards, forwards). Player 2 is on offense, player 1 is defense. The rules are:
1. Only three dribbles are allowed.
2. The ball is live until the coach calls dead ball.
3. One point per shot.
4. The game ends when the first player scores five points.
5. If you make a basket, offense stays, new defensive comes on.
6. Offense can rebound and put the shot back in the hoop.

COACHING POINTS: Work on dribbling with a purpose. Defense must block out and rebound. No flagrant fouls.

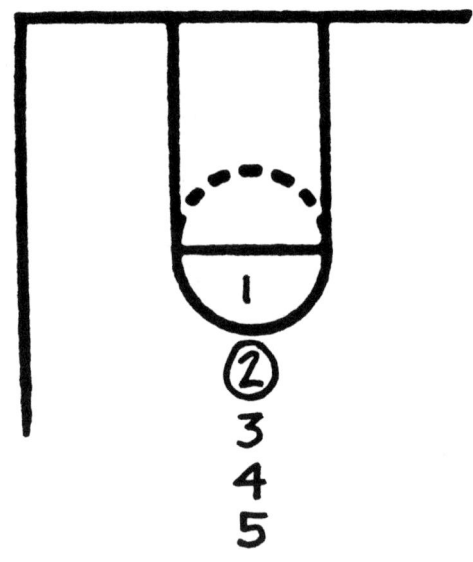

Name of Drill: TRANSITION "CLEAR"

Use throughout the season

PURPOSE: Teaches post players to run the break and get open for a shot on the low post block.

Line post players single file at half court. A coach is on the wing with a ball. On the word go, player 1 runs to the free throw line and fakes away, then calls "clear" and posts up on the low block. The coach will pass the ball to the post and the player will do a dropstep and shoot. Player 1 gets the rebound and throws it back to the coach. Every post runs through this drill twice and then the coach switches to the left side of the court.

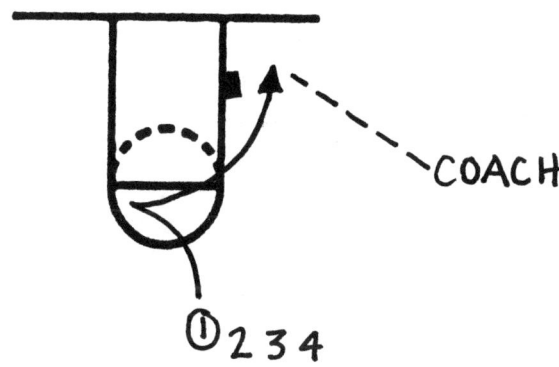

COACHING POINTS: Make sure the players fake away hard, then come strong and post up. To make the drill more advanced, put a coach on the block as a defensive player.

Name of Drill: ONE-ON-ONE HALF COURT
Use throughout the season

PURPOSE: To work on individual one-on-one moves and to work defense on the ball.

Divide the team into partners by position and quickness. Start the drill at half court with one player on offense and one on defense. The player with the ball is allowed a maximum of four dribbles. After a shot is attempted, both players go for the rebound. The drill is completed when a shot is made or the defense rebounds the ball. The players go to the end of the line and rotate offense to defense.

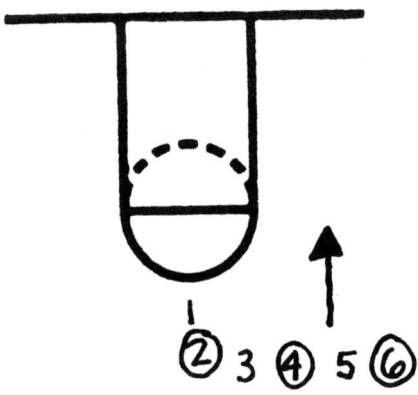

COACHING POINTS: Work on dribbling for a purpose. Read the defense. No flagrant fouls and box out.

Name of Drill: THREE PLAYER WEAVE/THREE SHOTS

Use pre-game warmup

PURPOSE: To loosen the team up during pre-game. Practice layups and jump shots.

Divide the team into groups of three at half court. The balls are in the middle line. Players 1, 2, and 3 perform the three player weave. Player 3 makes a bounce pass to player 1 and does a layup. Player 3's foot must now touch the sideline. Player 2 rebounds and passes to player 3 for a layup. Player 2 touches the sideline and receives a pass from player 1 for a layup. All three players go to the end of the line and players 4, 5, and 6 begin.

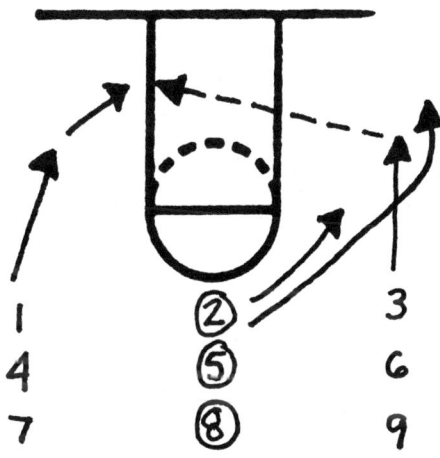

COACHING POINTS: Run hard and make good cuts to the basket. Perform the same drill with jump shots but no dribbling.

Name of Drill: THREE PLAYER SPOT SHOOTING
Use throughout the season

PURPOSE: Teaches to shoot from set spots on the floor.

Divide the team into groups of three at half court with the ball in the middle. Put two additional players on the baseline. Each baseline player should have a basketball. On the whistle, player 4 will chest pass to either player 5 or 3. When the pass comes back to the middle, the player will shoot a jump shot. Players 3 and 5 will crisscross and receive a pass from either player 1 or 2. They will shoot a bank shot with no dribble, rebound their own shot and become a passer on the baseline. Players 1, 2, and 4 will go back to half court.

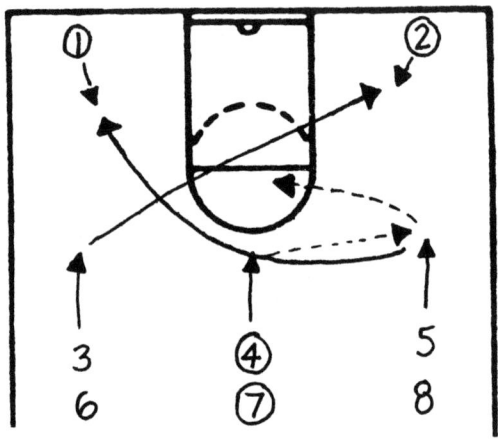

COACHING POINTS: Players will move and set themselves for good jump shots. Work on squaring to the basket.

Name of Drill: KNOCK-OUT SHOOTING
Use throughout the season

PURPOSE: Competitive and fun shooting drill.

Line the players up one behind the other at a basket. The first two players in line have a ball. On the whistle, the first player shoots and the second player in line can shoot immediately. The object of the game is for the player to put the shot in the basket before the person behind. Player 1 shoots and makes the basket and then passes to player 3. Player 2 misses and player 3 makes the basket before player 2 gets the rebound and follows. Player 2 is out of the game. The drill is over when only one player is left.

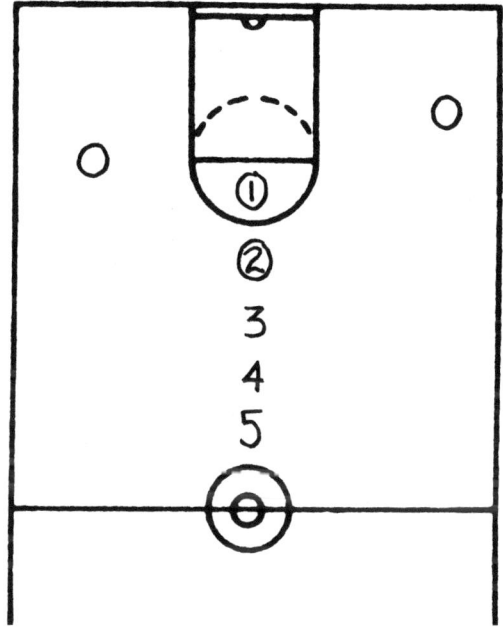

COACHING POINTS: If the player misses the shot, the player can rebound and put the ball in the hoop before the person behind the player. When the game is over, start the drill again on different spots on the floor (bank shots, three point shots).

Name of Drill: BREAKAWAY LAYUP DRILL
Use throughout the season

PURPOSE: Teaches the offensive player to go strong to the basket on a breakaway layup.

Divide the team into partners and put them on opposite corners of the court. They should be divided by speed and quickness. Player 2 has the ball and throws it out in front of player 1 who sprints and picks it up. Player 1 then dribbles the ball at fullspeed to score. Player 2 runs and tries to cut Player 1 off and play defense. At the same time, players 5 and 6 are dribbling and chasing going to the opposite basket. When the players complete their shots, they go to the end of the line and switch spots. The drill continues for a maximum of three minutes.

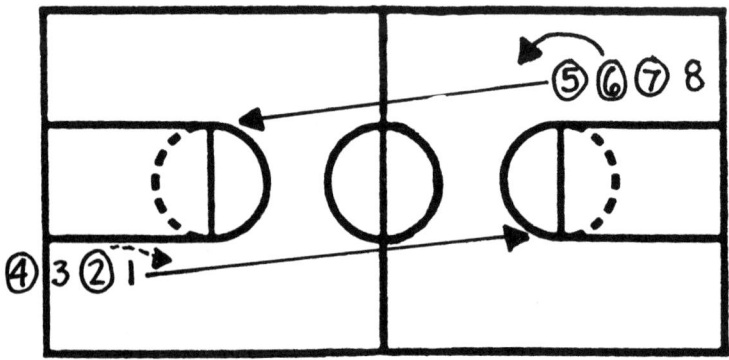

COACHING POINTS: This is an excellent drill for conditioning and teaching the offense to cut off the defense on a breakaway to the basket.

Name of Drill: THREE PLAYER CHASE AND SHOOT
Use throughout the season

PURPOSE: The drill improves the offensive players shooting with a hand in their face.

Divide the team into groups of three to a basket with one ball. Player A starts the drill by passing to player C. Player C is allowed to shoot immediately or take one dribble and shoot. After player A passes, player A will run toward player C and get a hand in player C's face and call "shot." After C shoots, C rebounds the shot and passes the ball to player B and puts a hand in B's face. The drill continues for three minutes.

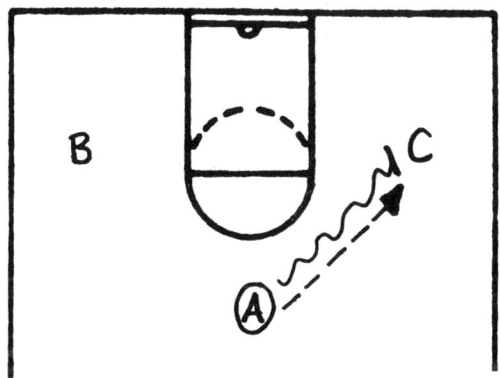

COACHING POINTS: Players A, B, and C can now move to any spot on the floor. Players are not allowed to block shots. This drill teaches the players to follow their shots.

Name of Drill: BEAT DR. "J" SHOOTING
Use throughout the season

PURPOSE: The drill creates a competitive atmosphere in shooting practice.

Divide the team into groups of two at separate baskets. Each player has a ball and is competing against themselves to try and beat Doctor "J." All shots are outside the key area and must all be made on the move. The game can be called at either 15 or 21. Every time a player makes a basket, they receive one point. Every time the players miss, Dr. J gets two points. The first to 15 or 21 wins the game.

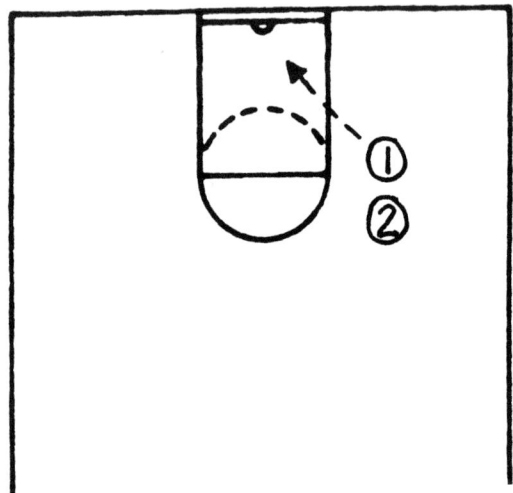

COACHING POINTS: This can be used as a team drill or an individual practice drill. It makes the players think before they shoot.

Name of Drill: "MIKAN" DRILL

Use throughout the season

PURPOSE: To improve hook shots.

Divide the team into partners at separate baskets. One ball should be at each basket. Player A will be under the basket and shoot a short right hand hook shot off the backboard with no dribble. Player A will rebound the shot and this time try the hook shot with the left hand. Shoot 10 shots and rotate partners. After each player shoots, do the same drill and dribble before shooting.

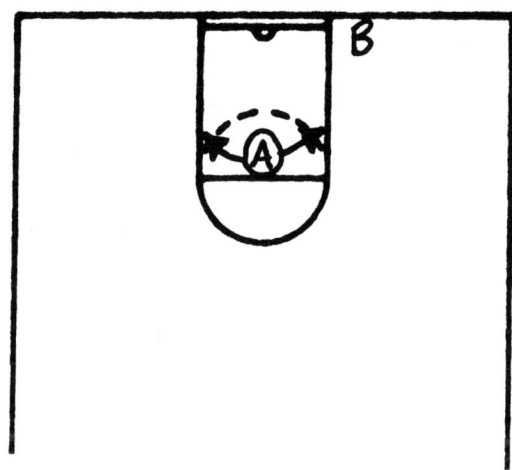

COACHING POINTS: Work with the players on getting the maximum height on their jump by kicking the knee up as high as possible.

Name of Drill: PARTNER FREE THROWS
Use throughout the season

PURPOSE: To put game pressure on the free throw shooter.

Divide the team into partners and send each group to a basket. Put five minutes on the clock or on a stopwatch. One player is the shooter and the partner rebounds. On the whistle, each shooter attempts a one-and-one. If she makes both shots, the partner will become the shooter. The new shooter will also attempt a one-and-one. If at any time the shooter misses, the player will dribble on a sprint to the oppositie baseline and dribble back. The player's partner will then become the shooter. Each player must make a preset number of free throws in five minutes. For example, the player must make 18 free throws. If the players don't make the preset number at the end of five minutes, those players not making the number must line up and run suicides for the missed number.

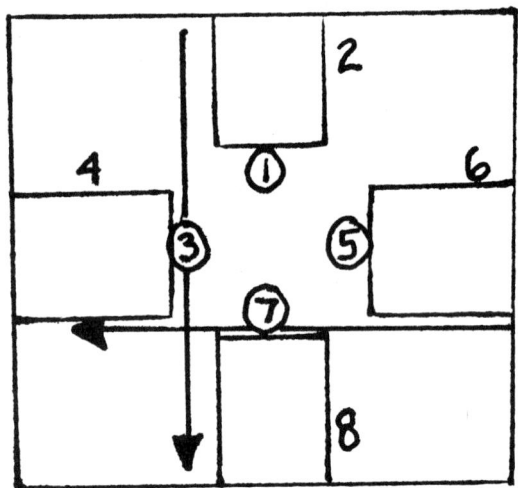

COACHING POINTS: Use the drill as a break in practice. Don't let the players rush their shooting. They need to take their time and concentrate.

Name of Drill: COMPETITIVE FREE THROWS

Use throughout the season

PURPOSE: Improves the free throw percentage.

Line the entire team around the free throw line area. Player 1 is at the free throw line and will attempt two free throws. Each player will rotate and shoot twice. Keep track of the number of free throws made. The coach will determine ahead of time a number that must be made. For example, 10 players shoot 20 shots, they must make 15. If they make 15 or more, the drill is over. If they make less than 15, the entire team runs a suicide for the missed number of free throws. If they only made 13 of 15 free throws, the team runs two suicides.

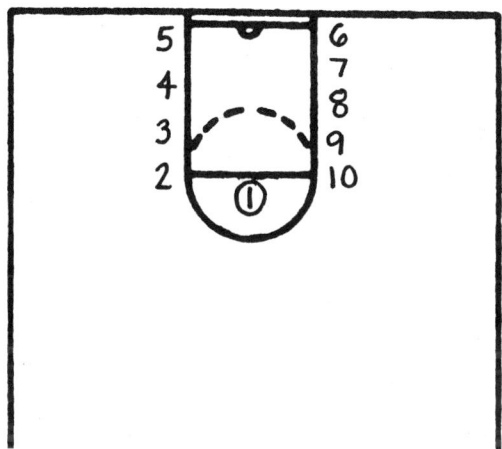

COACHING POINTS: Use this drill during practice or at the end of the day. Good for concentration while tired.

Name of Drill: TEAM FREE THROWS
Use throughout the season

PURPOSE: To improve free throws. Use this drill at the end of practice.

Line the entire team along the baseline. The first player in line goes to the free throw line to shoot. The player will shoot until a free throw is made. If the shot is made on the first attempt, the player will go to the end of the line. The next player in line will shoot. The entire team will run sprints according to the number of free throws missed. The drill is over once the entire team has shot.

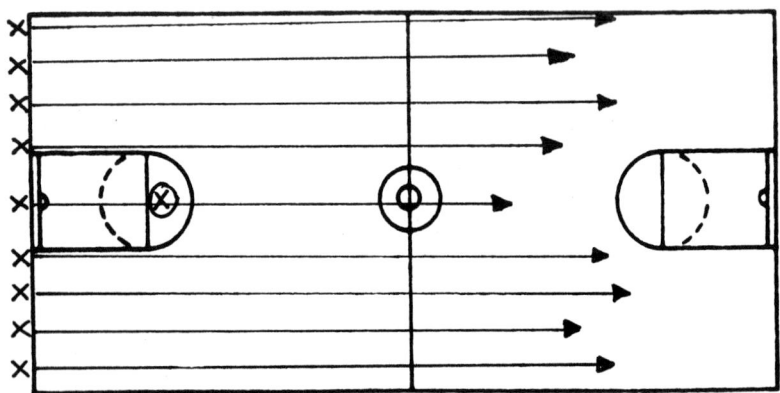

COACHING POINTS: Run sprints after each player finishes her round of shooting. Vary sprints with pushups, suicides, etc.

Name of Drill: REVERSE DRIBBLE/POWER LAYUP
Use throughout the season

PURPOSE: Improves ball handling and taking the ball strong to the basket.

Divide the team evenly into two lines. One line is the shooting line and the other one is the rebounding line. Give A and B balls. A will dribble to the corner baseline and will do a reverse dribble. A will continue dribbling and perform a power layup with the shoulders square to the basket protecting the ball with the body. The coach is under the basket to distract the player shooting by fouling the shooter or having hands up. The shooter then goes to the end of the line. Each player goes through the drill twice.

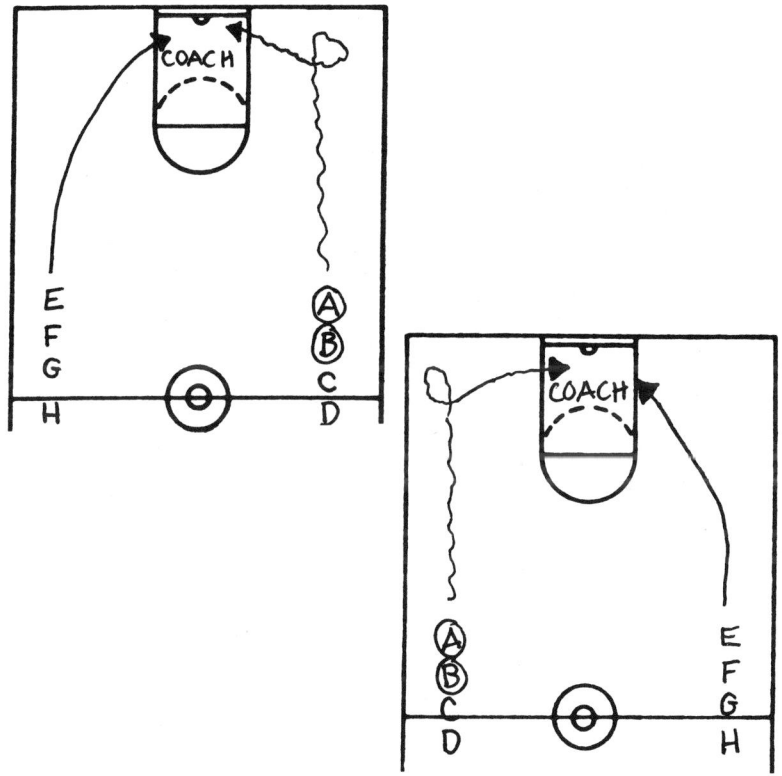

COACHING POINTS: When dribbling from the left side use your left hand. Shoot the ball with both hands and keep shoulders square to the basket.

Name of Drill: SHORT "17"

Use throughout the season

PURPOSE: Improves all phases of offensive basketball; ball handling, passing and shooting.

Divide the team evenly. Players with balls will be at the top of the key. A makes one or two dribbles going toward E who did a jump stop at the foul line corner. A passes to E, and now E has the following options.

1. Hand off ball to A for a give and go
2. Fake the hand off and take a jump shot
3. A can keep the dribble and use E as a screen and roll

The players go to the end of the opposite line when they are finished with the drill. Everyone goes through it twice.

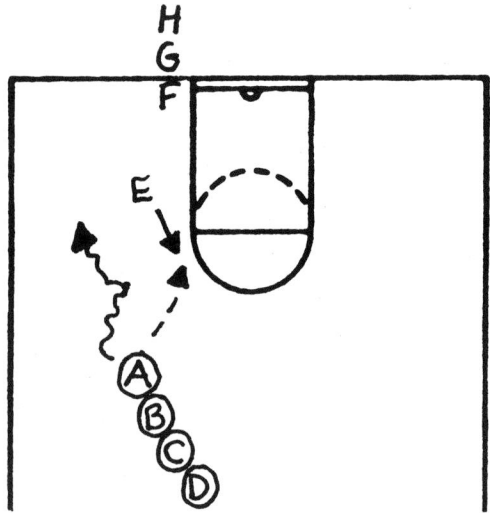

COACHING POINTS: The ball handler must make a hard cut to E and cut as close to E's shoulder as possible.

Name of Drill: TOSSBACK SHOOTING
Use throughout the season

PURPOSE: To improve the player's individual shooting technique.

Place the tossback on the wing with a line of players one behind the other with a ball. Each player will make a chest pass to the tossback and then make a move to the basket.

1. Square up, no dribble, jump shot
2. Square up, head fake, jump shot
3. Square up, fake left, dribble, jump shot
4. Square up, fake right, dribble, jump shot

After each player goes through each move twice, place the tossback on the opposite side of the court and repeat the drill.

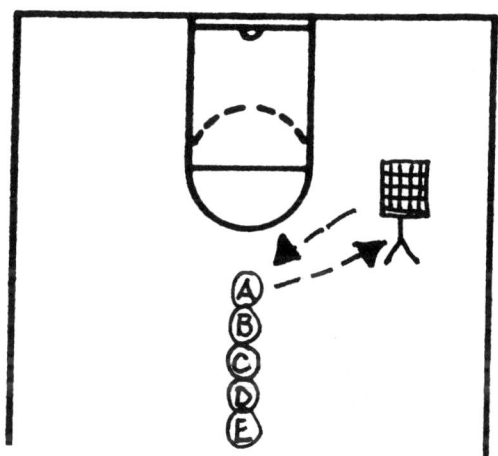

COACHING POINTS: Make sure the player uses the backboard when shooting from the wing.

Name of Drill: FULL COURT SHOOTING

PURPOSE: To improve shooting and passing on the move.

Divide the team into two lines of three players at one end of the court. At the other end of the court, have the players form at least two lines of two players. In the three player line, the middle player will have the ball. The first person in the two player lines each has a ball. Player B starts passing the ball to A and C. When the ball crosses midcourt, B dribbles the ball to the free throw line for a jump shot. A and C then receive a pass from G and H and shoot a jump shot from the wing. Then they get their rebound and go to the end of the line. B rebounds and passes downcourt to G and H until reaching half court. B then shoots a jump shot from the freethrow line while G and H receive passes from D and F for jump shots. When all the players are finished shooting, they go to the end of the line and a new three player line starts with E, D and F. Keep track of all baskets. The players must make 25 baskets in two minutes or less.

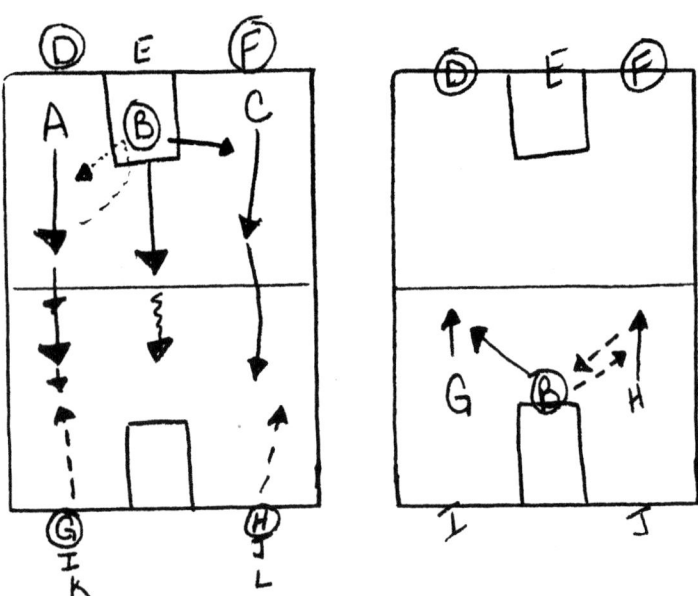

COACHING POINTS: Players need to be quick but without turnovers. The middle player shoots on the dribble and the wing players will shoot using the backboard without the dribble.

Name of Drill: BIG POST DRILL
Use throughout the season

PURPOSE: To help inside players learn to go strong to the basket.

Divide the team into groups of three by position. Place two balls on each block. Players A and B will rebound. Player C will shoot. On the whistle, C will pick up the ball and make a jump shot. B will rebound the ball. C will then move as quickly as possible to the next ball and shoot it. A will rebound that ball. The drill will last for 30 seconds. Each player keeps the total of the shots made. Players will then rotate.

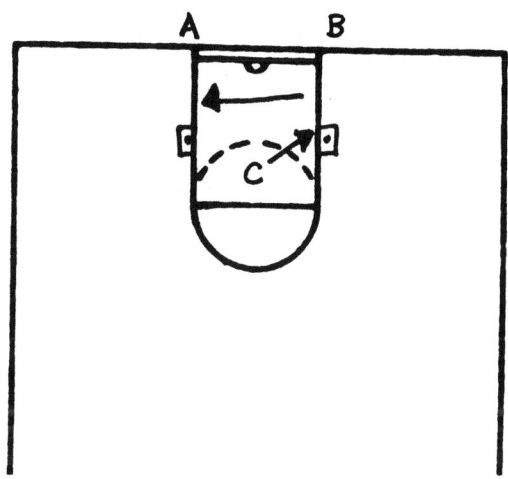

COACHING POINTS: This drill teaches the players to square their shoulders to the basket and to shoot with two hands.

Name of Drill: POST SHOOTING
Use throughout the season

PURPOSE: To help inside players develop their shots and individual moves.

Post player A will post on the block. Players B and C will position themselves on the wing with the ball. On the whistle, player B will pass to A who will post up, make a drop step without a dribble, and shoot. Player A will get the rebound and pass back to B. Player A will then cut across the key and post up. She will receive a pass from C and dropstep and shoot. This will continue for 10 shots and the players will rotate.

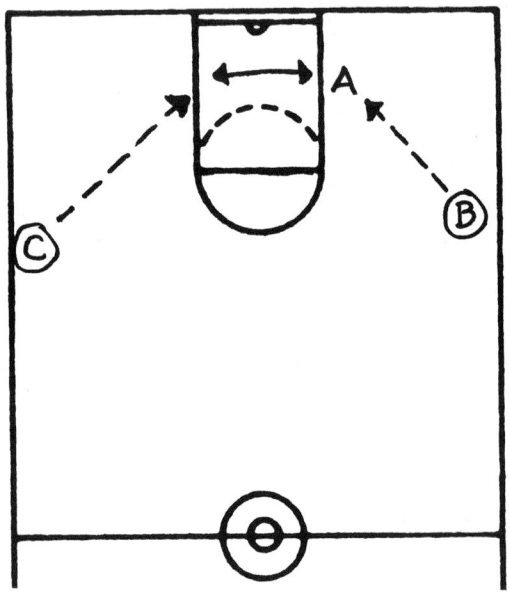

COACHING POINTS: The coach needs to decide on the moves. Dropstep without a dribble; dropstep, power dribble; square, fake, power dribble and dropstep to the middle are all options.

Name of Drill: CONTEST THE SHOOTER/REBOUND
Use throughout the season

PURPOSE: Teaches the shooter to release the ball with a hand in the face and follow the shot for a rebound.

Divide the team into teams of three by position. A, B, and C have basketballs and position themselves one behind the other behind the baseline. D, E and F are at the top of the key. A will pass to D. D cannot dribble until A is set for defense. D's options are a jump shot or take no more than two dribbles and shoot. A must play good defense and get a hand up when D shoots a jump shot. A will then blockout and get the rebound. The players will then go to the opposite line. When every player goes through twice, the shooting line moves to other spots on the court.

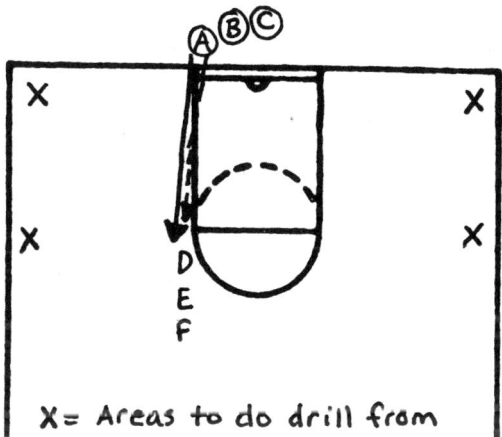

COACHING POINTS: Work with the offensive player on reading the defense before making a move.

Name of Drill: REACTION SHOOTING
Use throughout the season

PURPOSE: The reaction drill decides whether to use a quick jumper or dribble and make a move.

Divide the team evenly and go to both ends of the court. Line the players up. Each player has a ball and will dribble and chest pass to a coach at the top of the key. On the return pass back, the coach will yell "right" or "left." When the pass is received, the player must make a reaction dribble on the right or the left and a short jumper. If the coach says nothing on the return pass, the player will make a bank shot with no dribble. After the rebound, the player will go to the end of the opposite line.

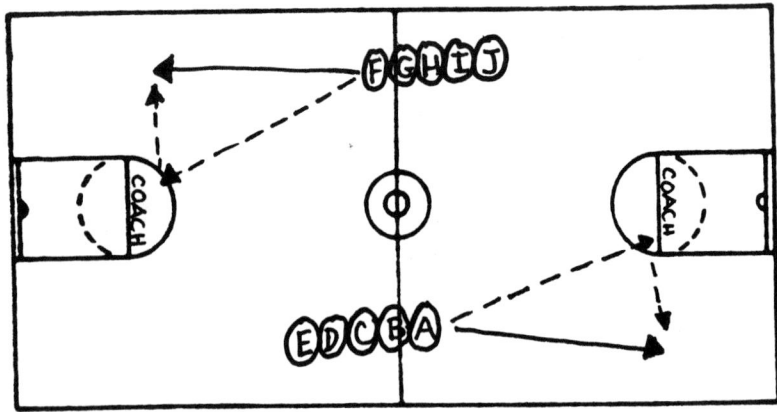

COACHING POINTS: Stress to make a good move and to square up to the basket.

Name of Drill: TWENTY-ONE

Use throughout the season

PURPOSE: To work on form, quick releases and to follow the shot for a rebound.

Divide the squad into pairs and send them to separate baskets. A has the ball and on command will shoot a jump shot from the wing. If the player makes the basket, the team gets two points. If the player misses and rebounds the ball before it touches the ground and tips it in, the player's team gets one point. (The player can also make the basket and get the ball out of the bucket and put it back in for a total of 3 points.) After the player completes the shot, the player will pass the ball to B and B will attempt the same shot. The first team to reach 21 points wins the game. The losing teams do pushups. When the drill is completed, move to another spot on the floor and start over again.

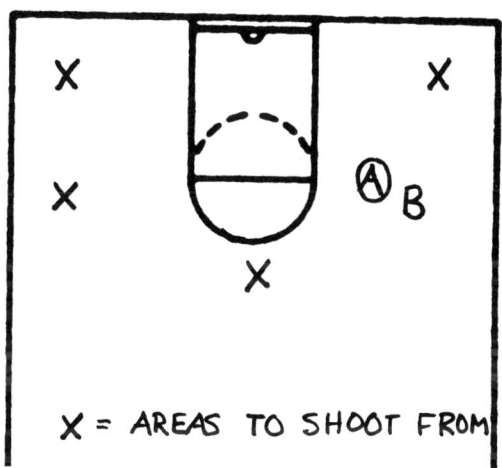

COACHING POINTS: No dribbling and shoot quickly. When shooting from the wing, only backboard shots count.

Name of Drill: THREE PLAYER/TWO BALL SHOOTING

PURPOSE: Jump shots with no dribble. Work on form and quick release.

Jump shots are taken as quickly as possible with no dribbling. A is the shooter, B is the passer and C is the rebounder. A will shoot from the baseline then move quickly to the wing position and receive a pass from B. After shooting, the player will move back to the baseline and receive another pass from B. The player will then shoot 10 shots and will then become the rebounder. B will become the shooter and C the passer. Each player will shoot 10 shots then do the same from the top of the key and from the opposite side of the court.

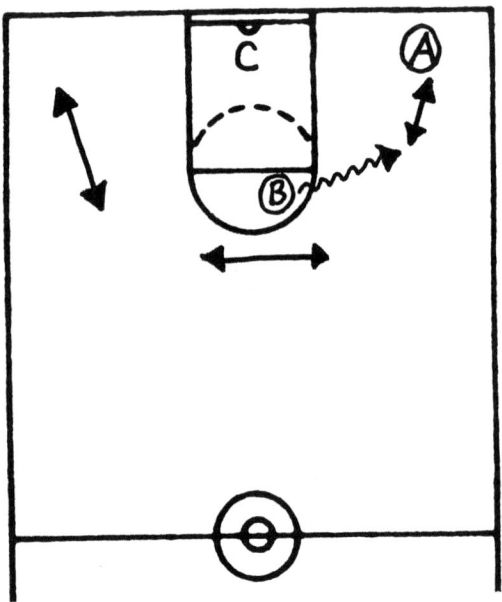

COACHING POINTS: Emphasize squaring to the basket and extension on release. Start with two balls.